Published by WonderWoof Publishers

Copyright © 2024 by Max Fetchwell

Printed and bound in the United States of America

First Printing

Table of Contents

Introduction

Welcome, curious readers, to the Wonderful World of Dogs! In this paw-some adventure, we are about to embark on a journey filled with wagging tails, heartwarming stories, and fascinating facts that are bound to bring a smile to your face.

Dogs, our furry friends, have a magical way of capturing our hearts with their boundless energy, loyalty, and playful antics. Get ready to discover the incredible world of these lovable creatures, as we dive into their unique features, intelligence, and heart-touching stories.

So, whether you're a dog lover or just looking for a reason to grin, join us on this exciting exploration into the canine wonders that make our world brighter and more joyful. Get ready for a tail-wagging adventure that will leave you with a heart full of happiness!

Let me tell you a bit about myself. I've adored dogs for as long as I can remember. When I was 6, my family got our first dog, and ever since, I've been all about dogs! My partner and I do lots of cool stuff with dogs, like search and rescue, carting (that's like draft work), tracking, and even programs where dogs visit people for comfort.

We've been in this dog world since 1983, and we have focused on keeping certain types of dogs, like Rottweilers, Shiba Inu, and Chihuahuas, in good shape and happy.

Welcome to the

Wonderful World of Dogs

Dogs are amazing creatures that have been our loyal companions for a very long time. These furry friends come in all shapes and sizes, from tiny Chihuahuas to giant Great Danes. Did you know that there are over 340 different breeds of dogs? Each one has its own special qualities and traits that make them unique.

A long time ago, people started to notice that dogs were really helpful. They helped with hunting, guarding, and even herding animals. As humans settled down and formed communities, they realized that dogs could be more than just helpful – they could be great companions too!

So, people began to choose dogs with specific traits that were useful for their needs. For example, if someone needed a dog to help herd sheep, they would pick dogs that were good at rounding up animals. Over time, this led to the creation of different dog breeds with unique skills and characteristics.

People started breeding dogs that had the traits they liked, such as size, coat type, and behavior. This process of selective breeding continued for many generations, and that's how we got the wide variety of dog breeds we have today.

In the 1800s, dog shows became popular for the evaluation of breeding stock. People began to showcase their dogs to see who had the best-looking and most well-behaved ones. This further encouraged the development of distinct breeds, as people aimed to create dogs that fit certain standards.

Nowadays, there are hundreds of dog breeds, each with its own history and purpose. Some breeds are excellent swimmers, some are great at retrieving, and others are perfect for being loving family pets. The history of creating different dog breeds is like a big puzzle, with each piece representing a unique story of humans working together with dogs to make the perfect companions.

One cool thing about dogs is their incredible sense of smell. While we humans have about 5 million smell receptors, dogs can have up to 300 million! That's like having a superpower for sniffing out interesting scents. This is why some dogs are trained to help find missing people or even detect certain diseases with their noses.

Dogs also have a special way of communicating with us. They use their tails, ears, and barks to express how they're feeling. For example, a wagging tail usually means they're happy, while a tucked tail might mean they're scared. Some dogs, like the Basenji, are known as "barkless" because they make a unique yodel-like sound instead of barking.

One fascinating fact is that dogs dream just like we do! Have you ever noticed your dog twitching or making small sounds while they're asleep? That's because they're in the middle of a dream adventure. It's like they have their own nighttime movies playing in their heads.

Whether they're showing us love with a slobbery kiss or keeping us company on a walk, dogs truly are our furry friends. Their loyalty, playfulness, and unique qualities make them special companions that bring joy and smiles to our lives. So, next time you see a dog, give them a pat on the head and remember all the wonderful things that make them such amazing members of our families.

Dogs' Unique Features

Amazing Nose Power

Imagine if you had a superhero nose, like our furry friends, the dogs! Dogs have noses that are super-duper amazing. Their sense of smell is so extraordinary that it's 10,000 to 100,000 times more sensitive than ours – that's like having a nose that can sniff out the smallest, hidden treasures.

Dogs use their incredible nose power for all sorts of cool things. One of their superhero tasks is finding lost items. Have you ever misplaced your favorite toy or couldn't find your socks? Well, a dog's nose could come to the rescue! They can sniff out scents and track down lost things with their fantastic smelling abilities.

But wait, there's more! Dogs aren't just great at finding stuff; they can also use their nose power for even bigger missions. Some specially trained dogs work with humans to detect illnesses. Yep, you heard it right – dogs can be like medical detectives! They can smell certain scents that humans can't, helping doctors figure out if someone is sick.

So, next time you see a dog sniffing around, remember that they are using their incredible nose power. It's like they have a magical tool that helps them explore the world and do some pretty amazing things. Dogs truly have noses that make them the superheroes of the smell world!

<u>Wagging Tails and Communication</u>

Did you know that dogs are like expert communicators, but instead of talking with words, they use body language? Yup, it's true! When dogs want to tell us something or share how they're feeling, they use their bodies in all sorts of cool ways.

One of the ways dogs talk to us is through their tails. Have you ever noticed how a dog wags its tail? Well, that's like their way of speaking without words. If a dog wags its tail happily and energetically, it usually means they're excited or joyful. But if their tail is low or tucked between their legs, it might mean they're a bit scared or unsure about something.

But tails aren't the only part of a dog's body that tells a story. Their faces are like expressive maps! Dogs use different facial expressions to show their feelings. When a dog is happy, their eyes might sparkle, and their mouth may turn up in what looks like a smile. On the other hand, if a dog is feeling scared or anxious, their ears might go back, and they might show their teeth a little.

Dogs don't just communicate with us; they also talk to each other using these cool body language tricks. So, next time you see a dog, pay attention to their tail wags and facial expressions – it's like they're trying to share their thoughts and feelings with us without saying a single word!

Doggy Intelligence

Doggy intelligence is a captivating aspect of our four-legged companions' cognitive abilities. Much like humans, dogs can display remarkable cleverness and acquire a wide array of skills. The term encompasses a spectrum of mental capacities, encompassing learning, memory, reasoning, and problem-solving. Dogs with high intelligence can swiftly comprehend commands, master new tricks, and navigate various situations with remarkable adaptability. The level and type of intelligence exhibited by different dog breeds can vary, influenced by factors such as genetics, training, and environmental stimulation. Recognizing and comprehending doggy intelligence is of utmost importance for effective training, communication, and fostering a strong bond between dogs and their human companions.

The intelligence of dogs unveils itself in various ways, extending beyond the realm of tricks and commands. While some dogs may swiftly learn tricks, the concept of intelligence in dogs delves deeper into their problem-solving skills and their ability to adapt to diverse situations. A dog that figures out how to open a door or ingeniously reaches a toy placed at a height demonstrates its problem-

solving prowess. Moreover, dogs exhibit an emotional intelligence that

enables them to understand human emotions. Many dogs excel at

sensing their owner's feelings, offering comfort, and providing

companionship when needed.

Certain dog breeds are often hailed for their exceptional

intelligence. The Border Collie and Poodle, for example, are

frequently regarded as highly intelligent due to their capacity to learn

new tasks and follow instructions adeptly. However, intelligence in

dogs is not solely confined to specific breeds; it is a trait that can be

nurtured and developed through training, interaction, and

environmental enrichment.

The role of training and quality time spent with dogs is pivotal

in the development of their intelligence. Engaging dogs in games,

presenting them with puzzles, and incorporating positive

reinforcement during training sessions are instrumental in stimulating

their minds and keeping them mentally agile. Dogs, being inherently

social animals, thrive on the companionship and interaction they share

with their human counterparts. This interaction not only deepens the bond between dogs and their owners but also contributes significantly to the cognitive development of the canine companions.

Moreover, understanding the factors that influence doggy intelligence aids in creating an environment that nurtures and supports their mental abilities. Genetics play a crucial role, as certain breeds may have a predisposition for specific cognitive traits. However, the impact of genetics can be enhanced or mitigated through appropriate training and environmental influences. A well-structured and stimulating environment, enriched with various sensory experiences, can contribute significantly to the cognitive well-being of dogs.

The multifaceted nature of doggy intelligence adds to the charm of our furry friends. Their ability to learn, reason, solve problems, and comprehend human emotions makes them not only adorable but also valuable members of our families. The unique combination of genetic predisposition, training, and environmental influences shapes the intelligence of each dog, creating a fascinating spectrum of cognitive abilities within the canine world.

Doggy intelligence is a multifaceted and captivating aspect of our canine companions. From learning tricks to solving problems and understanding human emotions, dogs exhibit a diverse range of cognitive abilities. The intelligence of dogs is not limited to specific breeds but is influenced by a combination of genetics, training, and environmental factors. Recognizing and appreciating doggy intelligence is essential for effective communication, training, and fostering a strong bond between dogs and their human companions. Through thoughtful training, engaging interactions, and a stimulating environment, we can enhance the cognitive well-being of our furry friends, making them not only lovable pets but also intelligent and responsive members of our families.

Variety of Breeds

Dogs come in so many different shapes, sizes, and personalities that it's like having a big menu of furry friends to choose from! Each dog breed is unique and special in its own way. Let's dive into the fascinating world of how dog breeds vary.

Imagine walking into a doggy playground, and you see dogs of all kinds – some big, some small, some fluffy, and some sleek. That's because there are more than 340 different breeds of dogs around the world! These breeds have been developed over many years for various purposes, such as herding, hunting, guarding, and just being great companions.

One way dogs vary is in their size. Picture a tiny Chihuahua that can fit in your pocket – it's like having a little ball of energy always ready to play. On the other end of the spectrum, there's the giant Great Dane, standing as tall as a grown-up person when they stretch up. Size doesn't just affect how much space they take up; it also influences their needs and how they interact with us. Small dogs may enjoy being carried or sitting on laps, while big dogs might need more

room to roam and play.

Have you ever seen a Border Collie perform incredible tricks?

Some dog breeds are known for being super smart and quick learners.

These brainy buddies can pick up on commands and tasks with ease.

The Border Collie, for example, is not just a fluffy friend but also a

helpful assistant around the house. They can learn to do all sorts of

tricks, making them the furry geniuses of the dog world.

Now, think about dogs that are known for their strength and

power, like the Siberian Husky. These dogs are like little furry

athletes, ready to pull sleds through snow-covered landscapes. Their

strength and endurance make them excellent workers in challenging

environments. It's fascinating how different breeds have unique

qualities that match their historical roles and jobs.

Skills and qualities don't stop at tricks or strength; they extend

to activities like swimming or herding. Some dogs, like the agile

Labrador Retriever, are natural swimmers. They love splashing in the

water, retrieving toys, and sometimes even rescuing people! On the other hand, herding dogs, like the Australian Shepherd, have a special talent for guiding and managing livestock. It's like having a furry friend who is not only a great companion but also a skilled worker.

Let's talk about appearances – the way dogs look. Some breeds are known for their long, silky fur, while others have short and sleek coats. The fluffy Pomeranian, for instance, looks like a little ball of fur with a big personality, while the smooth-coated Greyhound is all about grace and speed. The way a dog looks can tell us a lot about their breed and history.

Different breeds also have distinct features like ear shapes, tail lengths, and snout sizes. Bulldogs, with their unique wrinkled faces and pushed-in noses, have a look all their own. Meanwhile, the Dachshund's long body and short legs make them easily recognizable. These features not only contribute to a dog's appearance but also play a role in how they experience the world around them.

Have you ever thought about having a dog as a buddy who understands your emotions? Dogs are like emotional superheroes. They have an incredible ability to sense human feelings. If you're feeling happy, they might wag their tails and playfully bounce around. If you're a bit sad or scared, they might come over and offer comforting snuggles. It's like having a friend who can read your mind and is always there to share your joys and comfort you during tough times.

In the vast world of dogs, there's a breed for everyone. Whether you love big dogs, small dogs, fluffy dogs, or sleek dogs, each one brings its own bundle of joy and unique qualities. The next time you see a dog, take a moment to appreciate the amazing variety of breeds and the special things that make each one a one-of-a-kind furry friend. Dogs are not just pets; they are incredible companions, each with its own story and charm, waiting to become a special part of your life!

Heartwarming Stories

There are numerous heartwarming stories about dogs displaying extraordinary loyalty to their owners that have made headlines over the years. Here are a few notable examples:

<u>Buddy</u>

Buddy was the very first seeing eye dog! In the 1920s, a kind and smart German Shepherd named Buddy helped change the lives of people who couldn't see well. A wonderful woman named Morris Frank, who was blind, teamed up with Buddy's trainer, Dorothy Harrison Eustis. Together, they trained Buddy to guide Morris through the busy streets of New York City. Buddy learned to stop at curbs, avoid obstacles, and even cross the road safely. Thanks to Buddy's cleverness and loyalty, Morris gained more independence and confidence. Buddy paved the way for other amazing seeing-eye dogs, showing the world how these furry friends could be a helping paw for people with vision challenges.

Hachiko

Perhaps one of the most famous stories of canine loyalty is that of Hachiko, an Akita dog in Japan. Hachiko was best friends with his owner, Professor Ueno. Every day, Hachiko waited at the Shibuya train station for Professor Ueno to come back from work. They had a routine that made them really close. Sadly, one-day Professor Ueno didn't return, but Hachiko kept waiting for him at the station for a very long time, almost ten years. People in the town were so moved by Hachiko's loyalty that they built a statue in his honor at the station. Hachiko's story teaches us about the strong bond between pets and their owners and how love can last, even when someone we care about is no longer with us.

Fido in Italy

During World War II, a street dog named Fido in Italy became known for waiting at a bus stop every day for his deceased owner to return. Fido continued this routine for over 14 years until his passing. The heartwarming tale of Fido unfolds as a testament to the enduring bond between humans and animals. Fido, a stray dog, found an unexpected friend in a kind man named Carlo. Their friendship blossomed, leading Carlo to provide Fido with a loving home. This simple act of kindness transformed Fido's life, and he became a cherished member of Carlo's family. Fido's story resonates as an example of the positive impact individuals can have on the lives of stray animals, emphasizing the importance of compassion and companionship. In Italy, Fido's narrative is celebrated as a reminder that every act of kindness towards our furry friends can make a significant difference, turning a street dog into a beloved companion.

<u>Capitan in Argentina</u>

In 2006, a German Shepherd named Capitan captured attention when he stayed by his owner's grave in Argentina. Capitan reportedly followed the funeral procession to the cemetery and continued to visit the grave daily for years, displaying remarkable loyalty. Capitan's story began when he became a loyal companion to his owner, Miguel Guzmán. When Miguel passed away in 2006, Capitan displayed extraordinary loyalty by refusing to leave his owner's gravesite. Despite attempts to bring him back home, Capitan chose to stay by Miguel's side. The story of Capitan's unwavering devotion spread and people from all around were moved by his loyalty. Capitan's tale serves as a touching reminder of the deep bond between humans and their faithful canine friends, showcasing the extraordinary ways in which dogs can express love and companionship.

<u>Greyfriars Bobby</u>

In Scotland, the story of Greyfriars Bobby unfolds as a remarkable tale of loyalty. Greyfriars Bobby was a Skye Terrier who became famous in the 19th century for his unwavering devotion to his owner, John Gray. When John Gray passed away, Bobby continued to faithfully guard his owner's grave at Greyfriars Kirkyard in Edinburgh. Despite facing challenges, Bobby's loyalty remained steadfast, and he spent many years near the gravesite. The people of Edinburgh were deeply moved by Bobby's dedication, and his story became well-known. A statue of Greyfriars Bobby was erected near the cemetery to honor his loyalty, making him a symbol of faithful companionship. The tale of Greyfriars Bobby reminds us of the enduring bond between humans and their loyal canine friends, leaving an indelible mark on the hearts of those who hear his story.

<u>Kabang in the Philippines</u>

In the Philippines, there was a brave and heartwarming story about a mixed-breed dog named Kabang. In 2011, Kabang courageously saved two young girls from an oncoming motorcycle, but in the process, she suffered serious injuries to her snout and upper jaw. The community rallied together to help Kabang receive medical attention, and she underwent successful surgeries. Kabang's resilience and the compassion of those who cared for her touched the hearts of many, both locally and internationally. Her story became an inspiration, showcasing the deep connection between humans and animals. Kabang's journey is a testament to the kindness and empathy that can be found in communities, demonstrating the positive impact people can have on the lives of animals in need.

These stories showcase the deep bonds and loyalty that dogs can develop with their owners, often going to extraordinary lengths to express their devotion and companionship.

Heroic Acts

Numerous news stories have highlighted the heroic acts of dogs saving their owners or helping others. Here are a few remarkable dogs:

<u>Balto and the Serum Run</u>

Balto's heroic tale during the Serum Run of 1925 is an inspiring chapter in history. In the harsh Alaskan winter, a diphtheria outbreak threatened the lives of many, and the only way to save them was to transport antitoxin serum over 600 miles through treacherous conditions. Balto, a Siberian Husky, led a team of sled dogs through extreme cold and harsh weather, covering the final leg of the perilous journey. His determination and courage helped deliver the life-saving serum to the people of Nome, Alaska, preventing the spread of the deadly disease. Balto's bravery in the face of adversity showcases the crucial role that animals can play in times of crisis and underscores the powerful connection between humans and their loyal canine companions. The statue of Balto in New York City's Central Park stands as a lasting tribute to his remarkable contribution to the Serum

Run and his unwavering dedication to saving lives.

Laika, the Space Dog

Laika, the Space Dog, holds a significant place in history for

her pioneering journey into space. In 1957, during the early days of

space exploration, Laika became the first living creature to orbit the

Earth aboard the Soviet spacecraft Sputnik 2. Laika's mission paved

the way for human space travel and expanded our understanding of the

challenges animals face in space. While her journey was a

groundbreaking achievement, it also raised ethical concerns about the

treatment of animals in scientific experiments. Laika's courage and

sacrifice continue to be remembered, serving as a reminder of the

progress and responsibility that come with exploration. Though Laika

did not return from her mission, her contribution to space exploration

remains a symbol of the enduring spirit of discovery.

Trakr in the World Trade Center Rescue

Trakr, a brave and dedicated German Shepherd, played a

heroic role in the aftermath of the September 11, 2001 terrorist attacks

on the World Trade Center. Owned by police officer James

Symington, Trakr worked tirelessly as a search and rescue dog at Ground Zero. His keen sense of smell helped locate the last survivor, Genelle Guzman, trapped beneath the rubble. Trakr's courage and determination, along with the efforts of other rescue teams, brought hope and healing during a challenging time. Trakr's contribution to the World Trade Center rescue mission exemplifies the remarkable bond between humans and their service animals, showcasing the vital role these devoted companions play in times of crisis.

<u>Kelsey's 20-Hour Vigil</u>

Kelsey, a brave Golden Retriever, demonstrated extraordinary loyalty and resilience during a challenging situation. In 2019, Kelsey's owner suffered a severe medical emergency outside in freezing temperatures. Despite the harsh weather conditions, Kelsey stayed by her owner's side for a remarkable 20 hours, barking for help and providing warmth. Kelsey's unwavering vigil proved crucial, as a neighbor eventually heard the barks and called for assistance. The devoted actions of Kelsey highlight the remarkable bond between dogs and their owners, showcasing the powerful ways in which animals can act as protectors and companions during times of need. Kelsey's story serves as a touching reminder of the deep connection between humans and their faithful canine friends.

Daisy and the Burning House

In 2018, a remarkable Pit Bull named Daisy displayed incredible heroism by alerting her owner to a fire in their home. Sensing the danger, Daisy acted swiftly and persistently to wake up her owner and warn them about the growing threat. Thanks to Daisy's quick thinking and bravery, both the owner and Daisy were able to escape the house safely before the fire could cause harm. This courageous act not only showcased the intelligence and loyalty of dogs but also emphasized the valuable role they can play as protectors in our lives. Daisy's story serves as a powerful reminder of the special bond between humans and their canine companions and the life-saving instincts that our furry friends possess.

These stories demonstrate the remarkable courage, intelligence, and loyalty of dogs, showcasing how they can be true heroes in times of crisis or need.

Super Heros

Did you know that some dogs are like superheroes, trained to help people with disabilities? It's pretty amazing! These special dogs have awesome skills that make a big difference in people's lives.

Some dogs are trained to detect when a person is about to have a seizure. Imagine having a furry friend who can sense when something like that is about to happen and give you a heads up. It's like having a guardian angel with fur!

Other incredible dogs are trained to use their super sniffing powers to detect infections. Yep, you heard it right! These clever canines can smell changes in a person's body odor that might signal an infection. It's like having a four-legged health detective!

And that's not all – there are dogs trained to assist people who use wheelchairs or have trouble moving around. These dogs can fetch things, open doors, and even help with daily tasks, making life a bit easier for their human pals.

So, the next time you see one of these amazing assistance dogs, remember they are not just furry companions; they're like real-life superheroes, using their special talents to make the world a better place for their human friends.

Then some incredible dogs do really important jobs to help people. Have you ever heard about guide dogs? Well, guide dogs are amazing assistants for people who can't see well. They are like furry guides, helping their owners walk around safely and avoid obstacles. Imagine having a friend who knows all the best paths and helps you cross the street – that's what guide dogs do for visually impaired people.

Now, let's chat about therapy dogs. These are special dogs that bring lots of comfort and happiness to people in hospitals and schools. Picture a furry buddy coming to visit you when you're feeling a bit down or when you're in the hospital. Therapy dogs are like fluffy healers, making people smile and feel better. They're super good at giving cuddles and spreading cheer, making tough times a bit brighter.

So, whether it's helping someone find their way with guide dogs or bringing joy with therapy dogs, these furry pals are like heroes making the world a better place for everyone they meet!

Fun and Playful

Puppy Playtime! Ever wonder why puppies are always so playful and curious? Well, it's because they're like little adventurers, exploring their world and having loads of fun!

Puppies are like tiny scientists; they love to sniff, touch, and play with everything around them. It's how they learn about the big, exciting world they've just joined. Just like you explore new places and try new games, puppies use playtime to discover what they like and what makes them happy.

But guess what? Play isn't just about having a blast – it's super important for a puppy's health, both in their bodies and their brains. When puppies play, they're not just burning off energy; they're also getting exercise that keeps their bodies strong and healthy. It's like going to the gym but with lots of tail-wagging fun!

And here's the cool part – playtime is like a puppy's school for their brain. It helps them learn important stuff, like how to solve problems and socialize with other dogs and humans. Just like you learn math and make friends at school, puppies learn how to be awesome

doggy friends through play.

So, the next time you see a puppy bouncing around, remember,

they're not just goofing off – they're being little explorers and learners,

making sure they grow up to be happy and healthy doggy pals!

Unusual Dog Jobs

Did you know that dogs can have super cool jobs, just like people? Yep, it's true! Let's dive into the exciting world of doggy careers.

First up, we have truffle-hunting dogs. These clever canines have a nose for sniffing out truffles, which are fancy and delicious mushrooms that grow underground. The dogs use their amazing sense of smell to help chefs and farmers find these hidden treasures. It's like they have a secret talent for uncovering tasty treats!

Next, we have search and rescue dogs. These heroes are like four-legged detectives, helping find people who might be lost or in trouble. Their keen sense of smell and strong bodies make them perfect for sniffing out scents and navigating tricky places. They work with brave humans to save lives and bring comfort in challenging situations.

Now, let's talk about some furry celebrities! Yep, you heard it right – dogs can be famous too! Some lucky pups have careers in the entertainment industry, starring in movies and TV shows. They get to show off their acting skills and charm audiences around the world. It's like they have their red carpet-moments, stealing the spotlight with their adorable faces and wagging tails.

But wait, there's more! Dogs can also become therapy animals. These special friends visit hospitals, schools, and other places to spread joy and comfort. Their superpower? Making people smile and feel better with their furry presence. It's like having a cuddly friend right when you need it most.

Let's not forget about police dogs. These brave buddies work alongside police officers to keep communities safe. With their sharp senses, they can sniff out illegal stuff and track down bad guys. They're like the real-life superheroes of the doggy world, always ready to protect and serve.

Ever heard of assistance dogs? These amazing pals help people with disabilities in various ways. Some guide the visually impaired, while others assist those with mobility challenges. It's like having a furry sidekick that's always there to lend a helping paw.

Now, here's a job that's out of this world – astronaut dogs! Okay, maybe not exactly astronauts, but dogs have been part of space missions. They helped scientists understand the effects of space travel and zero gravity on living beings. It's like they had a little taste of being space explorers!

Last but not least, we have herding dogs. These clever canines work on farms, helping farmers manage and guide livestock. With their natural instincts, they can round up sheep or cattle with ease. It's like they're the farm's furry managers, keeping everything in order.

So, there you have it – dogs with jobs that range from truffle hunting to starring in Hollywood films. These furry pals show us that no matter their size or breed, dogs can have incredible careers that make a positive impact on the world!

Trivia

1. Dogs belong to the Canidae family, which also includes wolves, foxes, and other animals.

2. A dog's sense of smell is incredibly powerful; some breeds have up to 300 million smell receptors, compared to about 5 million in humans.

3. Research suggests that dogs experience similar sleep patterns and brain activity as humans, including the rapid eye movement (REM) stage associated with dreaming. If you've ever noticed your dog twitching or making little sounds while sleeping, they are likely dreaming.

4. Dogs have a remarkable ability to understand and respond to human emotions. They can sense their owner's mood and even demonstrate empathy. Studies have shown that dogs can differentiate between human facial expressions and respond accordingly.

5. Dogs can understand human gestures, including pointing. This is considered a sign of their social intelligence.

6. Tennis balls were initially designed for dogs as toys, not for the sport of tennis. They were later adapted for use in tennis after it was discovered that they were well-suited for the game.

7. Dogs have three eyelids. Dogs have an upper lid, a lower lid, and a third lid, known as a nictitating membrane or "haw," which helps keep the eye moist and protected.

8. Dogs Have Unique Nose Prints. Just like human fingerprints, each dog's nose has a unique pattern of ridges and creases. This nose print can be used to identify individual dogs. Before tattoos were used, individuals would ink and print their dog's nose on paper. This was used to record and identify them.

9. Tug-of-War Origin. The game of tug-of-war dates back to ancient times and was played by the ancient Greeks, Egyptians, and Romans, often using the form of a rope.

10. Dogs Have Sweat Glands in Their Paw Pads. Dogs don't sweat through their skin like humans. They release heat primarily through their paw pads and by panting. Dogs release a small amount of sweat through their paw pads, contributing to cooling their bodies.

11. Dogs have about 1,700 taste buds, while humans have around 9,000.

12. Webbed Feet. Some dog breeds, such as the Labrador Retriever and Rottweilers, have webbed feet, which makes them excellent swimmers.

13. A group of Pugs is called a "grumble."

14. Dalmatian puppies are born completely white and develop their iconic spots as they grow older.

15. The Chihuahua holds the title of the world's smallest dog breed. They often weigh less than 6 pounds (2.7 kg).

16. The Great Dane holds the record for the world's largest dog breed. Some individuals can reach over 30 inches (76 cm) tall at the shoulder.

17. The Saluki is considered one of the oldest dog breeds, with historical evidence dating back over 5,000 years.

18. The Greyhound is one of the fastest dog breeds and can reach speeds of up to 45 miles per hour.

19. Dog groomers dislike grooming the doodle breeds because their coats tend to matt so easily.

20. The Norwegian Lundehund is a dog breed with six toes on

each foot.

21. Dogs have a sense of time and can develop a routine. They

often know when it's time for meals or walks based on their

internal clock.

These trivia bits showcase the diverse and fascinating world of

dogs and their unique characteristics.

Uniqueness of Breeds

The Basenji is a special kind of dog that comes from Africa. One interesting thing about them is that they don't bark like most dogs. Instead, they make a cool sound called a "barroo." It's a bit like a yodel, which makes them stand out from other dogs. Basenjis are good at hunting because they have a strong sense of smell and are fast and agile. Photo by Edvinas Bruzas on Unsplash

The **Chihuahua** is a small and spirited dog breed known for its diminutive size, large eyes, and alert expression. Originating from

Mexico, these dogs are cherished for their loyalty and confidence despite their tiny stature. With a friendly and adaptable nature, Chihuahuas make charming and affectionate companions, demonstrating both courage and a big heart in their small bodies. Photo by Montclaire Chihuahuas

The **Dalmatian** is a distinctive and medium-sized dog breed recognized for its white coat adorned with black or liver-colored spots. Originating from Croatia, these dogs were historically used as carriage dogs. With a friendly and energetic nature, Dalmatians make excellent family pets, known for their unique appearance and playful personalities. Photo by Lorren & Loki on Unsplash

The **Great Dane** is a majestic and giant dog breed, known for its impressive size, sleek coat, and gentle temperament. Originating from Germany, these dogs were historically used for hunting large game. With a friendly and affectionate nature, Great

Danes make loyal family pets, showcasing both their imposing stature and a calm, gentle demeanor. Photo by Brad R on Unsplash

Photo by Maja Erwinsdotter on Unsplash

The **Saluki** is an elegant and ancient dog breed, recognized for its slim build, long legs, and distinctive smooth coat. Originating from the Middle East, these dogs were historically prized for their speed and endurance in hunting. With a graceful and gentle nature, Salukis make affectionate family companions, showcasing both their athletic prowess and a calm, dignified demeanor.

The **Norwegian Lundehund** is a dog breed with six toes on each foot. This unique feature helps them climb steep cliffs to hunt puffins. Originating from Norway, these clever and agile dogs were originally used for hunting puffins on steep cliffs. Photo: Alice Van Kempen

The **Greyhound** is a fast and sleek dog breed, known for its incredible speed and slender build. Originally bred for hunting and racing, Greyhounds are gentle and affectionate companions, often enjoying a good sprint followed by some relaxed lounging. A Greyhound Is Not Always Fast. Despite their reputation as fast runners, Greyhounds are often referred to as "couch potatoes" and are known for their calm demeanor indoors. Photo by Jannik Selz on Unsplash

With roots dating back thousands of years, the **Afghan Hound** is recognized as one of the oldest known dog breeds. This elegant breed is also celebrated for its opulent and flowing coat, adding to its distinctive charm and allure. Known for its dignified demeanor and distinctive appearance, the Afghan Hound boasts a regal posture contributing to its timeless elegance.

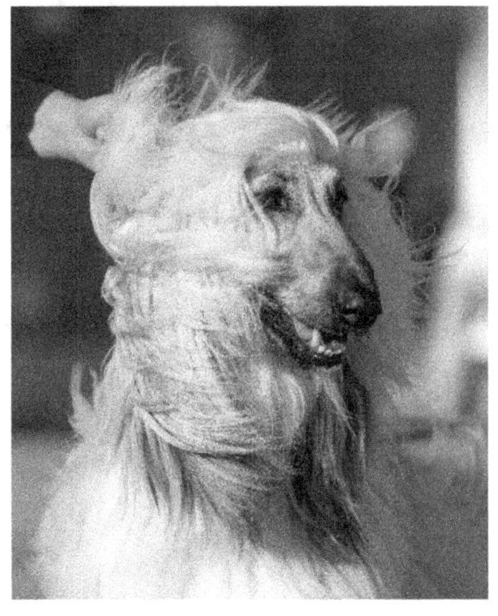

Photo by Mladen Šćekić on Unsplash

The **Shiba Inu** is a small and spirited dog breed from Japan, admired for its fox-like appearance, curled tail, and bold personality. Known for its intelligence and independence, the Shiba Inu makes a loyal and charming companion, bringing a touch of Japanese heritage and playful energy to its family.

Photo by Maxim Izbash on Unsplash

The **Alaskan Malamute** is a strong and friendly dog breed originally bred for pulling heavy sleds in the Arctic. With a thick coat, erect ears, and a powerful build, they are well-suited for cold climates and are known for their loyalty and endurance. The Alaskan Malamute's friendly nature extends to its pack mentality, making them excellent family dogs, while their expressive

eyes and sociable disposition further enhance their appeal as devoted companions. Photo by Josephine Amalie Paysen on Unsplash

The **Poodle** is an intelligent and elegant dog breed known for its curly, hypoallergenic coat. With a distinctive appearance and a friendly temperament, Poodles come in different sizes, including standard, miniature, and toy, making them adaptable and suitable for various living environments.

Photo by Ezequiel Garrido on Unsplash

The **Beagle** is a small and friendly breed of dog recognized for its distinctive long ears, short legs, and keen sense of smell. Beagles are often used as scent hounds

in tasks such as hunting and detection due to their strong olfactory abilities and amiable nature.

Photo by Jaspal Kahlon on Unsplash

The **Chow Chow** is a unique and dignified dog breed, known for its distinctive lion-like mane and blue-black tongue. Originally from China, these dogs have a reserved and independent temperament, making them loyal and protective companions. Photo by Freysteinn G. Jonsson on Unsplash

The **Border Collie** is an intelligent and energetic dog breed, recognized for its exceptional herding abilities. With a medium-sized frame, expressive eyes, and a smooth or rough coat, Border Collies are known for their agility and trainability, making them excellent working dogs and loyal family pets. Photo by Will Gardiner on Unsplash

The **Basset Hound** is a charming and low-to-the-ground dog breed, known for its long ears and distinctive, droopy expression. With a keen sense of smell and a calm demeanor, Basset Hounds are often used for tracking scents and make affectionate companions with their gentle nature. Photo by Apostolos Vamvouras on Unsplash

The **New Guinea Singing Dog** is a rare and primitive dog breed native to the mountainous regions of Papua New Guinea. With a unique vocalization resembling a melodious song, these dogs are known for their agility and adaptability to the challenging environment they inhabit, making them a fascinating and distinct canine breed. Photo: Cole Bearcat

The **Havanese** is a small and cheerful dog breed, originally from Cuba, distinguished by its silky, wavy coat and expressive eyes. Known for their friendly and sociable nature, Havanese dogs make wonderful companions and are often referred to as "Velcro dogs" due to their affectionate tendency to stick close to their owners. Photo: Alice Van Kempen

The **Shetland Sheepdog**, also known as the Sheltie, is an intelligent and agile dog breed with a thick double coat, often showcasing a distinctive mane and frill. Originally bred as herding dogs in the Shetland Islands, these dogs are not only adept at agility but also make devoted and gentle family companions with their friendly demeanor. Photo by Kim Eggler on Unsplash

The **Pomeranian** is a small and lively dog breed, characterized by its fluffy double coat and fox-like expression. Despite their diminutive size, Pomeranians are known for their bold and confident personalities. With a friendly disposition, these charming dogs make delightful companions and can adapt well to various living environments. Photo by Bennet Robin Fabian

The **Jack Russell Terrier** is a small and energetic dog breed, recognized for its distinctive white coat with tan or black markings.

Known for their intelligence and agility, these terriers were originally bred for hunting. With a lively spirit and a friendly demeanor, Jack Russell Terriers make affectionate pets and excel in various canine activities due to their quick wit and boundless energy. Photo by Glen Carrie on Unsplash

The **Komondor** is a large and unique dog breed with a corded, mop-like coat that protects from the elements. Originating from Hungary, these dogs were traditionally used as livestock guardians. With a calm and steady temperament, Komondors are known for their loyalty and protective instincts, making them excellent guardians and devoted companions.

Photo by Margarita Marushevska on Unsplash

The **Dachshund** is a small and long-bodied dog breed with a distinctive shape and short legs. Originally bred for hunting, these dogs are known for their courage and determination. With a friendly and curious nature, Dachshunds make loving family pets and are recognized for their loyalty and spirited personalities.

Photo by James Watson on Unsplash

The **Siberian Husky** is a medium-sized dog breed known for its thick double coat, erect triangular ears, and distinctive markings. Originating from Siberia, these dogs were initially bred by the Chukchi people for sledding and endurance. Huskies are friendly, and energetic, and make great family pets with their sociable nature and striking appearance.

Photo by Ayush Madikunt on Unsplash

The **Boxer** is a medium to large-sized dog breed, recognized for its strong, muscular build and distinctive square-shaped head.

Originally developed in Germany, these dogs are known for their loyalty, intelligence, and playful nature. With a short coat and a friendly demeanor, Boxers make excellent family companions and are often appreciated for their protective instincts. Photo by Lucie Helešicová on Unsplash

The **Australian Shepherd** is a medium-sized herding dog known for its intelligence, agility, and striking merle coat patterns. Originally developed in the United States, despite the name, these dogs are highly versatile and excel in various activities. Australian Shepherds are loyal, energetic, and make devoted companions with their friendly nature and eagerness to work closely with their owners. Photo by Martin Blanquer on Unsplash

The **Bulldog** is a medium-sized dog breed with a distinctive wrinkled face, muscular build, and pushed-in nose. Known for their gentle and calm demeanor, Bulldogs were originally bred for bull-baiting in England. Today, they are cherished for their loyalty and make excellent companions, especially for families, due to their affectionate nature. Photo by Sébastien L. on Unsplash

The **Whippet** is a slender and graceful dog breed, similar in

appearance to a small Greyhound. Known for their speed and agility, Whippets were originally bred for racing and hunting in England. With a gentle and affectionate temperament, these dogs make loving companions and are appreciated for their elegant yet athletic build. Photo by Dada Mar on Unsplash

The **Pug** is a small and charming dog breed with a distinctive wrinkled face, curled tail, and friendly expression. Originally from China, these dogs were prized companions of Chinese emperors. With a playful and affectionate nature, Pugs make delightful

family pets and are known for their loyalty and love for human companionship. Photo by Mink Mingle on Unsplash

The **Old English Sheepdog** is a large and shaggy dog breed known for its profuse, weather-resistant coat and distinctive "Bobtail" appearance. Originally bred in England for herding, these dogs are characterized by their gentle and good-natured temperament. With a playful and affectionate nature, Old English Sheepdogs make wonderful family pets and are recognized for their enduring loyalty. Photo by Ben Griffiths on Unsplash

The **Rhodesian Ridgeback** is a distinctive dog breed known for the "ridge" of hair along its back that grows in the opposite direction to the rest of its coat. Originally bred in Southern Africa for

hunting and guarding, these dogs are characterized by their strength, courage, and loyalty. With a calm yet protective nature, Rhodesian Ridgebacks make excellent family companions and are known for their independence and endurance. Photo by Ilona Frey on Unsplash

The **Shih Tzu** is a small and elegant dog breed with a luxurious, long, flowing coat and a distinctive pushed-in face. Originally bred as a companion dog for Chinese royalty, Shih Tzus are known for their friendly and affectionate nature. With a lively spirit and a calm demeanor, these dogs make delightful family pets, providing companionship and joy to those around them. Photo by Shikhar Bhatnagar on Unsplash

The **Maltese** is a small and elegant dog breed known for its long, silky white coat and friendly demeanor. Originating from the Mediterranean island of Malta, these dogs were cherished as companions by royalty and aristocrats. With a lively and affectionate nature,

Maltese make wonderful family pets, offering both companionship and a charming presence. Photo: Four Halls Maltese Perm Reg'd

The **Irish Wolfhound** is a giant and noble dog breed, originally bred in Ireland for hunting wolves and guarding estates. Known for their imposing size, rough coat, and gentle disposition, Irish Wolfhounds are often considered gentle giants. With a calm and friendly nature, they make loyal family companions, showcasing both strength and a warm heart. Photo by Stéphane Juban on Unsplash

The **Scottish Terrier**, commonly known as the "Scottie", is a small and sturdy dog breed with a distinctive wiry coat and erect ears. Originating from Scotland, these dogs were initially bred for hunting and burrow exploration. With a determined and spirited personality, Scottish Terriers make loyal and loving companions, valued for their independence and affectionate nature. Photo by Rowen Smith on Unsplash

The **Leonberger** is a large and majestic dog breed known for its impressive mane, friendly demeanor, and strong build. Originating in Germany, these dogs were initially bred as working and companion animals. With a gentle and sociable nature, Leonbergers make excellent family pets, offering both loyalty and a calm presence. Photo by Stephanie Lucero on Unsplash

The **Cocker Spaniel** is a medium-sized dog breed recognized

for its luxurious, wavy coat and long, pendulous ears. Originally bred for hunting in England, these dogs are known for their friendly and affectionate nature. With a joyful and gentle temperament, Cocker Spaniels make wonderful family pets, valued for their loyalty and adaptability.

Photo by David Berler on Unsplash

The **Bichon Frise** is a small and cheerful dog breed with a fluffy, curly coat and a charming, round face. Originating in the

Mediterranean, these dogs were historically favored by royalty and nobility. Known for their playful and affectionate nature, Bichon Frises make delightful companions, bringing joy and warmth to their families. Photo by Viktor Talashuk on Unsplash

The **Bullmastiff** is a large and powerful dog breed, recognized for its muscular build, short coat, and vigilant expression. Originally developed in England as a guard dog, these dogs are known for their courage and loyalty. With a calm and gentle demeanor, Bullmastiffs make devoted family pets, combining strength with a loving nature.

Photo by Albert Dávid on Unsplash

The **Keeshond** is a medium-sized dog breed known for its

thick double coat, distinctive "spectacles," and fox-like expression. Originating from the Netherlands, these dogs were historically companions to Dutch barge captains. With a friendly and outgoing nature, Keeshonds make excellent family pets, bringing both companionship and a lively spirit to those around them.

Photo: Amanda Lougheed

The **Australian Cattle Dog** is a medium-sized, sturdy dog breed, known for its intelligence, agility, and distinctive blue or red speckled coat. Originating from Australia, these dogs were developed for herding cattle. With a loyal and energetic nature, Australian Cattle Dogs make excellent working dogs

and companions, showcasing both versatility and a strong sense of loyalty. Photo by Daniel Lincoln on Unsplash

The **Papillon** is a small and elegant dog breed recognized for

its butterfly-like ears and fine, silky coat. Originating from France, these dogs were favored by European royalty. With a lively and friendly temperament, Papillons make delightful companions, offering both charm and agility in their petite stature.

Photo by River Fx on Unsplash

The **Wire Fox Terrier** is a small and energetic dog breed

known for its distinctive wiry coat and keen expression. Originally bred for fox hunting in England, these dogs are characterized by their intelligence and determination. With a lively

and friendly nature, Wire Fox Terriers make spirited companions and are admired for their agility and alertness. Photo: Alice Van Kempen

The **Xoloitzcuintli**, often referred to as the Mexican Hairless Dog, is a unique and ancient breed known for its hairless appearance

and loyalty. Originating from Mexico, this dog has been cherished by various civilizations throughout history, and its distinctive feature is the absence of a coat, making it stand out among other breeds. With a calm and affectionate nature, the Xoloitzcuintli makes a wonderful companion and is considered a symbol of Mexican culture and heritage. Photo: Alice Van Kempen

The **Entlebucher Mountain Dog** is a Swiss herding dog known for its compact size, tricolor coat, and strong work ethic. Originally bred for herding cattle in the Alps, this breed is recognized for its intelligence and agility. With a loyal and energetic nature, the Entlebucher Mountain

Dog makes a dedicated family companion, embodying both a strong sense of responsibility and a friendly disposition. Photo: Alice Van Kempen

The **Bergamasco Sheepdog** is a distinctive and intelligent breed originating from Italy, known for its corded coat that forms mats, giving it a unique appearance. This herding dog is valued for its

agility, keen instincts, and devotion to its flock. With a calm and gentle demeanor, the Bergamasco Sheepdog makes a loyal and effective working companion, reflecting its

historical role in guarding and herding livestock in the Italian Alps.

Picture Credit: Vanessa Lassin Photography/Getty Images)

The **Thai Ridgeback** is a unique and ancient dog breed originating from Thailand, recognized for the distinct ridge of hair along its back. With a loyal and independent nature, this breed was historically used for hunting and guarding. The Thai

Ridgeback is admired for its agility and endurance, making it a valuable companion for various tasks in its native land.

Photo: American Kennel Club

The **Canaan Dog** is a remarkable and ancient breed with roots in the Middle East, celebrated for its intelligence and adaptability.

Originally used for herding and guarding, this dog possesses a loyal nature and a strong sense of independence. The Canaan Dog's history and versatility make it a unique and valued companion, well-suited for various roles throughout the ages.

Photo: Genevieve Landis

The **Canadian Eskimo Dog** is a sturdy and ancient breed originating from the Arctic regions of Canada, known for its strength, endurance, and resilience in harsh climates. Originally used by the indigenous Inuit people for sledding and hunting, this dog is characterized by its dense double coat and erect ears. With a

loyal and friendly temperament, the Canadian Eskimo Dog remains an important part of northern heritage, embodying adaptability and hardiness. Photo: Alice Van Kempen

The **Lagotto Romagnolo** is a unique and affectionate dog breed hailing from Italy, recognized for its curly coat and truffle-

hunting abilities. With a friendly and playful nature, this breed has a history as a skilled retriever, particularly in wetlands. The Lagotto Romagnolo's versatility, coupled with its charming appearance, makes it a cherished companion, especially appreciated for its loving disposition and dedication to its family. Photo: Bridget Flynn

The **Catalburun** is an exceptional pointing dog from Turkey, distinguished by its unique split nose and strong hunting instincts. Known for its keen sense of smell and agility, this rare breed has a history deeply rooted in Turkish hunting traditions. With its distinct appearance and hunting prowess,

the Catalburun is esteemed for its abilities and remains a symbol of heritage and skill in its native land. Photo: Richard Trevor Wilson

The **Azawakh** is an elegant and swift dog breed originating from Africa, recognized for its slim physique and distinctive

appearance. Bred by nomadic tribes for hunting and guarding, the Azawakh is known for its speed, endurance, and loyalty. With a calm yet alert nature, this breed makes a devoted companion, embodying both grace and resilience in its role as a valued companion and protector. Photo: Deanna Vout

The **Cirneco dell'Etna** is a small and agile dog breed from Sicily, known for its slender build, large ears, and short coat.

Originally bred for hunting, this breed exhibits both speed and endurance. With a friendly and independent nature, the Cirneco dell'Etna makes a loyal family companion, combining its hunting heritage with a loving temperament. Photo: Lucia Prieto

The **Puli** is a Hungarian herding dog distinguished by its

distinctive corded coat, which resembles a mop. Known for its agility and intelligence, this breed was traditionally used for herding livestock. With a lively and devoted nature, the Puli makes a charming and affectionate companion, displaying both a unique appearance and a strong sense of loyalty to its family.

Photo: Alice Van Kempen

The **Irish Water Spaniel** is a versatile and water-loving dog breed, originating from Ireland and recognized for its curly, water-

resistant coat. Historically used for retrieving game from water, this breed is known for its intelligence and enthusiasm for outdoor activities. With a friendly and playful temperament, the Irish Water Spaniel makes a loving family pet, combining a love for water with a loyal and affectionate nature.

Photo: Alice Van Kempen

The **Chinook** is a rare and versatile American sled dog breed, known for its strength, friendly demeanor, and distinctive tan coat.

Developed in New Hampshire, this breed is prized for its endurance and adaptability to harsh climates. With a gentle and loyal nature, the Chinook makes an excellent family companion, showcasing both a working heritage and a loving temperament. Photo: American Kennel Club

The **Kuvasz** is a Hungarian livestock guardian breed known for its majestic appearance, strength, and protective instincts. With a dense, white coat and a history dating back centuries, this breed was traditionally used to guard livestock and estates. Known for its loyalty and calm demeanor,

the Kuvasz makes a devoted family companion, combining regal stature with a gentle nature. Photo: Kuvasz Club of Canada

The **Briard** is a French herding dog with a long, wavy coat, distinctive bushy eyebrows, and a loyal temperament. Bred for herding

and guarding, this ancient French breed is known for its intelligence and agility. With a devoted and protective nature, the Briard makes an excellent family companion, combining its herding heritage with a gentle and affectionate demeanor. Photo: Dogs in Design

The **Thai Bangkaew Dog** is a versatile breed from Thailand, recognized for its thick double coat and proficiency in herding and guarding tasks. With a loyal and protective nature, this breed has been an integral part of Thai culture. The Thai Bangkaew Dog's distinctive appearance and keen

instincts make it a cherished and valuable companion, embodying both a strong work ethic and a loving disposition. Photo: vttps://thaibangkaew.webnode.hu/szallas/

The **Tibetan Mastiff** is a large and powerful dog breed originating from Tibet, known for its thick mane, imposing size, and

protective instincts. Historically used to guard livestock in the Himalayas, this breed is characterized by its loyalty and independence. With a calm yet vigilant nature, the Tibetan Mastiff makes a formidable guardian and a devoted family companion, combining strength and a gentle temperament. Photo: Alice Van Kempen

The **Peruvian Inca Orchid** is a unique and ancient hairless dog breed from Peru, known for its elegant appearance and smooth skin. With a history dating back to Inca times, this breed was valued

for its companionship and hunting skills. The Peruvian Inca Orchid's distinctive beauty and friendly nature make it a cherished and prized companion, embodying both historical significance and a warm, affectionate demeanor.

Photo: American Kennel Club

Conclusion

We've taken a delightful journey through the paw-some world of dogs! From their extraordinary sense of smell to the way they wag their tails, dogs have proven to be incredible companions and friends.

We've explored the vast intelligence found in various breeds, from the playful and curious to the astoundingly clever Border Collies. Dogs, with their ability to learn commands and even understand our emotions, truly make our lives brighter.

The heartwarming stories of loyal companionship and the heroic acts of these furry friends have touched our hearts. Whether they're saving their owners or providing comfort as service dogs, dogs show us the true meaning of loyalty and friendship.

We've laughed and smiled at the playful trivia, from puppy playtime to the unusual jobs dogs take on. Their joyous energy and the variety of roles they play in our lives make them truly special.

So, let's celebrate these incredible creatures who bring immeasurable joy into our lives. Whether they're sniffing out scents, wagging their tails in excitement, or simply being by our side, dogs remind us of the pure happiness that comes from embracing the

wonderful world of our furry friends. Take a moment to appreciate the

paw-some wonders of dogs, and let their love continue to brighten

your days!

If you found this book helpful, I'd be very appreciative if you left a favorable review for the book on Amazon!

Resources

Smith, J. (n.d.). *Off the Leash Dog Cartoons | Off the Leash - 10 heartwarming dog stories from history*. http://offtheleashdogcartoons.com/scoops/10-heartwarming-dog-stories-from-history/

Fraga, K. (2023b, November 30). *11 famous dogs who earned the title of "Man's Best Friend."* All That's Interesting. https://allthatsinteresting.com/famous-dogs

Lisa, A. (2022b, September 21). 10 heartwarming stories about dogs saving humans' lives. *Good Good Good*. https://www.goodgoodgood.co/articles/dogs-that-saved-lives

Sabah, D. (2018, February 21). *Loyal Argentine dog dies beside owner's grave after 12 years of waiting there for him*. Daily Sabah. https://www.dailysabah.com/life/2018/02/21/loyal-argentine-dog-dies-beside-owners-grave-after-12-years-of-waiting-there-for-him

Reisen, J. (2021, June 24). *Dog Heroes: 10 Real-Life Tales of Heroic dogs*. American Kennel Club. https://www.akc.org/expert-advice/lifestyle/real-life-tales-of-heroic-dogs/#:~:text=Named%20one%20of%20history's%20most,of%20the%209%2F11%20attack.

Team, D. (2024, January 17). *The story of Kabang, the hero dog who lost her snout*. Dogster. https://www.dogster.com/lifestyle/kabang-hero-dog-philippines

Today, S. R. U. (2013, September 27). USA TODAY. *USA TODAY*.

https://www.usatoday.com/story/news/nation/2013/09/27/pit-bill-saves-

family/2884811/

Arnold, B. (2024, January 5). 6 Dogs that forever changed the course of human

history - The Dogington Post. *The Dogington Post*.

https://www.dogingtonpost.com/6-dogs-that-changed-the-course-of-history/

New Guinea singing dog. (2024, January 4). In *Wikipedia*.

https://en.wikipedia.org/wiki/New_Guinea_singing_dog

About TBD□:: *thaibangkaew*. (n.d.). Thaibangkaew.

https://thaibangkaew.webnode.hu/szallas/

Clancy, M. (2023, May 8). *Bergamasco Sheepdog*. DogTime.

https://dogtime.com/dog-breeds/bergamasco-sheepdog

ChatGPT. (n.d.). https://chat.openai.com/

Additional Resources

Websites for Further Learning

Canadian Kennel Club - https://www.ckc.ca/en/Choosing-a-Dog

American Kennel Club - https://www.akc.org/dog-breeds/